MINIMAL STYLE

MINIMAL

Exteriors   Interiors

STYLE

Details

EDITOR **Angelika Taschen**

TASCHEN

KÖLN LONDON LOS ANGELES MADRID PARIS TOKYO

Front cover: Ice age: glacial atmosphere in the old part of Lucerne.
Couverture : Âge de glace : ambiance glacier dans un loft de la vieille ville, à Lucerne.
Umschlagvorderseite: Eiszeit: Gletscher-Ambiente in einem Loft in Luzerns Altstadt.
Architect: Gus Wüstemann
Photo: Bruno Helbling/zapaimages

Back cover: A favourite place: Armand Bartos's stone bathtub.
Dos de Couverture : Coin préféré : la bai-gnoire de pierre d'Armand Bartos.
Umschlagrückseite: Lieblingsplatz: Die steinerne Badewanne von Armand Bartos.
Architect: Claudio Silvestrin
Photo: Deidi von Schaewen

Also available from TASCHEN:

Mies van der Rohe
96 pages
ISBN-13: 978-3-8228-3643-9; ISBN-10: 3-8228-3643-5 (English edition)
ISBN-13: 978-3-8228-3642-2; ISBN-10: 3-8228-3642-7 (French edition)
ISBN-13: 978-3-8228-2857-1; ISBN-10: 3-8228-2857-2 (German edition)

To stay informed about upcoming TASCHEN titles, please request our magazine
at www.taschen.com/magazine or write to TASCHEN, Hohenzollernring 53, D-50672 Cologne,
Germany, contact@taschen.com, fax: +49-221-254919. We will be happy to send you a free copy
of our magazine which is filled with information about all of our books.

Concept and editing by Angelika Taschen, Berlin
Layout and general project management by Stephanie Bischoff, Cologne
Texts by Christiane Reiter, Hamburg
Lithography by Thomas Grell, Cologne
English translation by Isabel Varea, Grapevine Publishing Services, London
French translation by Anne Charrière, Croissy/Seine

Printed in Italy
ISBN-13: 978-3-8228-2386-6
ISBN-10: 3-8228-2386-4

CONTENTS SOMMAIRE INHALT

Minimalism is the perfect counterpoint to the overstimulating effects of Modernism – which it predates by many years. Even in buildings of the Romanesque, Renaissance and Neoclassical periods we can spot minimalist tendencies (although they were not called that at the time). And Mediterranean and especially Zen-inspired Far Eastern architecture is simple and unadorned, in other words "minimalist". With architects like Walter Gropius and Mies van der Rohe, the Bauhaus was a milestone in the history of Minimalism. The term "Minimalism" came into widespread use in the 1960s. At that time it was used to define a new trend on the American art scene, characterised by a kind of rationality and a reduction to fundamentals which distanced it from more extravagant forms of expression such as Pop Art. Minimalism developed steadily and spread into other fields of artistic activity, graphic arts and design, fashion and film, literature and music – and also

REDUCE TO THE MAX
Christiane Reiter

Le minimalisme est le contrepoint parfait à une modernité qui nous bombarde de stimulations et d'excitations. Pourtant il a existé longtemps avant elle. Des tendances minimalistes sont déjà perceptibles dans les constructions romanes, renaissantes et néoclassiques (même si on ne les appelait pas encore ainsi à l'époque). L'architecture méditerranéenne, et surtout celle d'Extrême-Orient inspirée par la philosophie zen, a toujours été sobre et pure – minimaliste. Le Bauhaus, avec Walter Gropius et Ludwig Mies van der Rohe, a également été une étape dans l'histoire du minimalisme. Le concept de « minimalisme » n'est devenu populaire que dans les années 60. A l'époque, il désignait une nouvelle tendance de l'art moderne américain, qui se distinguait par une sobriété absolue et un réductionnisme radical de formes de représentation plus opulentes comme le Pop Art. « Phénomène en progression », le minimalisme a ensuite étendu son champ d'action au graphisme, au design, à la mode, au cinéma, à la littérature, à la musique – ainsi qu'à

Minimalismus ist der perfekte Kontrapunkt zur reizüberfluteten Moderne – und war schon lange vor ihr da. Bereits in Bauten der Romanik, der Renaissance und des Neoklassizismus kann man minimalistische Tendenzen erkennen (die nur damals noch nicht so genannt wurden). Die mediterrane und vor allem die von der Zen-Philosophie inspirierte fernöstliche Architektur sind seit jeher schlicht und puristisch – minimalistisch. Das Bauhaus mit Walter Gropius und Ludwig Mies van der Rohe war ein Meilenstein in der Geschichte des Minimalismus. Der Begriff »Minimalismus« wurde aber erst in den 1960ern populär. Damals bezeichnete er eine neue Tendenz in der amerikanischen Kunstszene, die sich mit Hilfe absoluter Nüchternheit und radikaler Reduktion von üppigeren Darstellungsformen wie der Pop Art abgrenzte. Der Minimalismus entwickelte sich stetig weiter und dehnte sein Wirkungsfeld aus: auf Grafik und Design, Mode und Film, Literatur und Musik – und auf die Architektur. Diese griff minimalistische Ansätze längst vergangener Epochen wieder auf

architecture. Architects reverted to the minimalist approaches of the distant past and revisited the minimalist ideas of the great master builders who were regarded as the founding fathers of Modernism. The first part of this book is devoted to such great names as Adolf Loos and his manifesto Ornament and Crime. Another is Ludwig Mies van der Rohe, who, with projects like the Barcelona Pavilion and Farnsworth House, redefined the concept of space. Among others featured are Le Corbusier and Louis I. Kahn, who at La Jolla created an aesthetic of empty space, and Richard Neutra, who in California built homes in the districts of Hollywood known ironically as "Badlands". Modern Minimalists like Luis Barragán, and later Tadao Ando, John Pawson and Claudio Silvestrin, had unlimited resources on which to draw. They then put all these ideas together and channelled them into the creation of Minimal Architecture to maximum effect.

l'architecture. Celle-ci a repris des tendances minimalistes d'époques parfois très anciennes, et s'est souvenue des idées minimalistes d'architectes éminents, considérés comme les « pères fondateurs de la modernité ». La première partie de ce livre est consacrée à des grands noms de ce type : Adolf Loos, avec ses constructions et son manifeste « Ornement et crime » ; Ludwig Mies van der Rohe, dont les œuvres telles que le Pavillon de Barcelone ou la Maison Farnsworth redéfinissent le concept d'espace ; Le Corbusier et Louis I. Kahn qui inventa à La Jolla une esthétique du vide ; Richard Neutra, enfin, qui créa en Californie ses habitats fascinants au cœur des paradis holly-woodiens, « ironiquement » surnommés les « Badlands » (mauvaises terres). Des minimalistes modernes comme Luis Barragán, et après lui Tadao Ando, John Pawson ou Claudio Silvestrin, puisent donc déjà dans un vaste patrimoine, recueillent des impressions, les canalisent et créent un « art minimal » avec effet maximal.

und erinnerte sich an minimalistische Ideen großer Baumeister, die als »Gründungsväter der Moderne« gelten. Solch großen Namen ist der erste Teil dieses Bandes gewidmet – Adolf Loos mit seinen Bauten und seiner Schrift »Ornament ist ein Verbrechen« sowie Ludwig Mies van der Rohe gehören zu ihnen, dessen Werke wie der Barcelona Pavillon oder das Farnsworth House den Begriff des Raums neu definierten. Ebenso Le Corbusier und Louis I. Kahn, der in La Jolla eine Ästhetik der Leere schuf, sowie Richard Neutra, der in Kalifornien mit Wohnwelten in den ironisch »Badlands« genannten Hollywood-Paradiesen faszinierte. Moderne Minimalisten wie Luis Barragán und später Tadao Ando, John Pawson oder Claudio Silvestrin schöpfen also aus dem Vollen – sie sammeln all diese Eindrücke, kanalisieren sie und schaffen »minimal architecture« mit maximaler Wirkung.

"… Less is more …"

Ludwig Mies van der Rohe

« … Moins c'est plus … »

Ludwig Mies van der Rohe

»… Weniger ist mehr …«

Ludwig Mies van der Rohe

EXTERIORS

Extérieurs   Aussichten

10/11 Multi-levelled: a house built by Adolf Loos between 1912/1913 in Vienna. *En escalier : maison d'habitation construite par Adolf Loos en 1912/13 à Vienne.* Abgestuft: Ein von Adolf Loos 1912/13 erbautes Wohnhaus in Wien.

12/13 A white cube: the Master's House, Dessau, built for Lyonel Feininger. *Cube blanc : maison de maître personnelle de Lyonel Feininger, à Dessau .* Ein weißer Würfel: Das Meisterhaus Feininger in Dessau.
Architect: Walter Gropius (1926/28)

14/15 Representing the nation: German Pavilion at the International Exhibition, Barcelona. *Représentatif : le pavillon allemand à l'exposition universelle, Barcelone.* Repräsentativ: Deutscher Pavillon auf der Weltausstellung, Barcelona. *Architect: Ludwig Mies van der Rohe (1929)*

16/17 Living in style: L.C. van der Vlugt's Sonneveld House in Rotterdam (1929/33). *Habiter avec style : la maison Sonneveld à Rotterdam , L. C. van der Vlugt (1929/33).* Stilsicher wohnen: Das Haus Sonneveld in Rotterdam von L. C. van der Vlugt (1929/33).

18/19 Like a translucent cube: The Boevé Villa in Rotterdam. *Comme un cube dé traversé de lumière : la maison Boevé à Rotterdam.* Wie ein lichtdurchlässiger Würfel: Das Haus Boevé in Rotterdam. *Architect: L. C. van der Vlugt (1931/33).*

20/21 Twins: two houses side by side in the Werkbund settlement in Vienna. *Maisons jumelles : dans le lotissement viennois de l'Association des artisans.* Im Zwillingslook: Doppelhaus in der Wiener Werkbundsiedlung. *Architect: Adolf Loos (1931)*

22/23 A new perception of space: Farnsworth House in Illinois. *Un nouvelle sensation de l'espace : la maison Farnsworth dans l'Illinois.* Ein neues Raumgefühl: Das Farnsworth House in Illinois. *Architect: Ludwig Mies van der Rohe (1945/50)*

24/25 A star of the 20th century: Richard Neutra's Kaufmann House in Palm Springs (1947). *Une star du XXᵉ siècle : la maison Kaufmann de Richard Neutra à Palm Springs (1947).* Ein Star des 20. Jahrhunderts: Richard Neutras Kaufmann House in Palm Springs (1947).

26/27 Cruciform ground plan and natural stone façade: the Kronish House in Beverly Hills. *Plan en croix et façade de pierre naturelle : la maison Kronish à Beverly Hills.* Kreuzförmiger Grundriss und Naturstein-Fassade: Das Kronish House in Beverly Hills. *Architect: Richard Neutra (1955)*

28/29 A meeting place for artists and intellectuals: the Chuey House, Los Angeles. *Lieu de rencontre des artistes et des intellectuels : la maison Chuey, Los Angeles (1956).* Treffpunkt der Künstler und Intellektuellen: Chuey House, Los Angeles. *Architect: Richard Neutra (1956)*

30/31 Aesthetics and functionality combined: buildings in La Jolla, California. *Esthétiques et fonctionnelles : les constructions à La Jolla, en Californie.* Ästhetisch und funktional zugleich: Bauten im kalifornischen La Jolla. *Archtiect: Louis I. Kahn (1959/65)*

32/33 Completely surrounded by water: Pierre Koenig's (1960) Case Study House No. 21. *Tout entourée d'eau : la maison Case Study House N° 21 de Pierre Koenig (1960).* Vollständig von Wasser umgeben: Das Case Study House No. 21 von Pierre Koenig (1960).

34/35 Steel frames and panoramic window: Pierre Koenig's (1960) Case Study House No. 21. *Cadre d'acier et fenêtres Bellevue : la maison Case Study House N° 21 de Pierre Koenig (1960).* Stahlrahmen und Bellevue-Fenster: Pierre Koenigs (1960) Case Study House No. 21.

36/37 Exhibition hall: Berlin's Neue Nationalgalerie. *Hall d'exposition : la nouvelle Nationalgalerie à Berlin.* Ausstellungshalle: Die Neue Nationalgalerie in Berlin. *Architect: Ludwig Mies van der Rohe (1965/68)*

38/39 Linked to the Naoshima Contemporary Art Museum: the Benesse House. *En liaison avec le Musée d'art contemporain de Naoshima : la maison Benesse.* Verbunden mit dem Naoshima Contemporary Art Museum: Das Benesse House. *Architect: Tadao Ando (1988/95)*

40/41 A new interpretation of Japanese tradition: the Forest Floor House. *Tradition japonaise revisitée : la Forest Floor House de Kengo Kuma.* Japanische Tradition neu interpretiert: Das Forest Floor House. *Architect: Kengo Kuma (2001/03)*

42/43 Like a chess board: the travertine walls of the Lotus House. *Damier : les murs en travertin de la maison Lotus.* Schachbrettartig: Die Travertinwände des Lotus House. *Architect: Kengo Kuma (2005)*

"… I don't believe that architecture should talk too much …"

Tadao Ando

« … Je ne pense pas que l'architecture doive trop en dire … »

Tadao Ando

»… Ich glaube nicht, dass Architektur zu viel reden sollte …«

Tadao Ando

INTERIORS

Intérieurs   Einsichten

48/49 Somewhere to stretch out: Barcelona daybed at Farnsworth House in Illinois. *Pour s'allenger : lit de jour Barcelone dans la maison Farnsworth , Illinois.* Hingestreckt: Barcelona-Tagesbett im Farnsworth House in Illinois. *Architect: Ludwig Mies van der Rohe (1945/50)*

50/51 Completely at one with nature: open-plan rooms at the Farnsworth House. *Harmonie avec la nature : pièces ouvertes dans la maison Farnsworth.* Harmonie mit der Natur: Offen gestaltete Räume im Farnsworth House. *Architect: Ludwig Mies van der Rohe (1945/50)*

52/53 Minimalism and luxury combined: dining room at the Farnsworth House. *Minimaliste et généreuse à la fois : salle à manger de la maison Farnsworth.* Minimalistisch und opulent zugleich: Esszimmer des Farnsworth House. *Architect: Ludwig Mies van der Rohe (1945/50)*

54/55 Straight lines: dining room in the Casa Luis Barragán built in 1947 in Mexico City. *Lignes rectilignes : salle à manger de la Casa Luis Barragán de 1947 à Mexico City.* Ganz geradlinig: Esszimmer in der Casa Luis Barragán von 1947 in Mexiko City.

56/57 Luminous: bright pink wall in the Casa Luis Barragán (1947). *Lumineux : mur rose bonbon, dans la Casa Luis Barragán (1947).* Leucht-kraft: Wand in kräftigem Pink in der Casa Luis Barragán (1947).

58/59 Limestone bench: in the living room of architect John Pawson's home in London. *Banc en pierre calcaire : dans le salon de la maison londonienne de l' architecte John Pawson.* Eine Sitzbank aus Kalkstein: Im Wohnzimmer des Londoner Hauses von Architekt John Pawson.

60/61 Separated only by a wall of glass: John & Catherine Pawson's kitchen and garden. *Séparés par une simple paroi de verre : cuisine et jardin de John & Catherine Pawson.* Nur durch eine Glaswand getrennt: Küche und Garten von John & Catherine Pawson.

62/63 Focus on material and form: unclut-tered spaces at John Pawson. *Concentration sur le matériau et la forme : des pièces d'un style puriste, dans la maison de John Pawson.* Konzentration auf Material und Form: Puristisch gehaltene Räume bei John Pawson.

64/65 The name says it all: in Tadao Ando's 4x4 House every room measures 4x4 meters. *Nom évocateur : dans la maison 4x4 de Tadao Ando, chaque pièce mesure quatre mètres sur quatre.* Nomen est omen: In 4x4 House von Tadao Ando misst jeder Raum 4x4 Meter.

66/67 Concrete, wood and glass: the clean lines of the kitchen in the 4x4 House *Béton, bois et verre : cuisine au design clair, dans la maison 4x4.* Beton, Holz und Glas: Die klar designte Küche im 4x4 House. *Architect: Tadao Ando (2003)*

68/69 An almost monastic atmosphere: a simple bedroom in the 4x4 House. *Atmo-sphère quasi monacale : chambre à coucher dans la maison 4x4.* Fast klösterliche Atmo-sphäre: Ein schlichtes Schlafzimmer im 4x4 House. *Architect: Tadao Ando (2003)*

70/71 Bath with a view of wooded hills: in Kengo Kuma's Lotus House. *Se baigner avec vue sur les montagnes et la forêt : dans la mai-son Lotus de Kengo Kuma.* Baden mit Blick auf bewaldete Berge: Im Lotus House von Kengo Kuma.

72/73 A magical moment: the pool in front of Kengo Kuma's Lotus House seen at twilight. *Un moment magique : bassin au crépuscule, maison Lotus de Kuma.* Ein Moment voller Magie: Das Wasserbassin vor Kengo Kumas Lotus House in der Dämmerung.

74/75 Free-floating stone steps: the Lotus House in Kamakura. *Marches de pierre suspendues : maison Lotus à Kamakura.* Frei schwebende Steinstufen: Im Lotus House in Kamakura. *Architect: Kengo Kuma (2005)*

76/77 Light as air: spiral staircase in Kengo Kuma's Lotus House. *Légèreté absolue : escalier en colimaçon, comme un filigrane, dans la maison Lotus de Kengo Kuma.* Absolute Leichtigkeit: Eine filigrane Wendeltreppe im Lotus House von Kengo Kuma.

78/79 Spectacularly spacious: a living and dining room designed by Vincent van Duysen. *Surfaces pleines d'effet : salon et salle à manger de Vincent van Duysen.* Wirkungsvolle Flächen: Ein Wohn- und Esszimmer, gestaltet von Vincent van Duysen.

80/81 Bare necessities: minimalist design by Vincent van Duysen. *Aucun accessoire superflu : design puriste de Vincent van Duysen.* Kein unnötiges Accessoire: Puristisches Design von Vincent van Duysen.

82/83 Shadow play: on the wall of a van Duysen kitchen. *Jeux d'ombres : au mur d'une cuisine signée Duysen.* Schattenspiele: An der Wand einer van-Duysen-Küche.

84/85 Pure white: bathroom designed by Vincent van Duysen. *D'une blancheur immaculée : une salle de bain dessinée par Vincent van Duysen.* Reines Weiß: Badezimmer-Design von Vincent van Duysen.

86/87 Open spaces: Forest Floor House has an air of fragility. *Pièces ouvertes : une apparence de fragilité, dans la Forest Floor House.* Offene Räume: Im fast zerbrechlich wirkenden Forest Floor House. *Architect: Kengo Kuma (2001/03)*

88/89 Contrasts: the minimalist interior and lush exterior of the Forest Floor House. *Contrastes : intérieur minimaliste et extérieur foisonnant, dans la Forest Floor House.* Gegensätze: Minimalistisches Interieur und üppiges Exterieur im Forest Floor House. *Architect: Kengo Kuma*

90/91 Brightly polished: kitchen floor at the London home of the architect Voon Yee Wong. *Il brille : le sol de la cuisine, dans la maison londonienne de l'architecte Voon Yee Wong.* Auf Hochglanz gebracht: Küchenboden im Londoner Haus des Architekten Voon Yee Wong.

92/93 Three-legged: eight kitchen stools stand in line. *Sur trois pieds : huit tabourets de cuisine bien alignés.* Auf drei Beinen: Acht Küchenhocker in Reih und Glied. *Architect: Voon Yee Wong*

94/95 All in order: open shelving at the London home of the architect Voon Yee Wong. *En ordre : systèmes d'étagères ouvertes dans la maison londonienne de l'architecte Voon Yee Wong.* In Ordnung: Offene Regalsysteme im Londoner Haus des Architekten Voon Yee Wong.

96/97 Interesting patterns: the kitchen of Tom de Paor's Double House in Dublin (2005). *Motif raffiné : la cuisine dans la maison jumelle de Dublin, Tom de Paor (2005).* Raffiniert gemustert: Die Küche im Double House in Dublin von Tom de Paor (2005).

98/99 Black and white: kitchen and living room in the Casa M-Lidia at Montagut. *Impressions en noir et blanc : cuisine et salon dans la Casa M-Lidia à Montagut.* Schwarz-weiß: Küche und Wohnzimmer in der Casa M-Lidia in Montagut. *Architect: RCR Arquitectes*

100/101 Light source: kitchen and living room in the Casa M-Lidia, designed by RCR Arquitectes. *A la source de la lumière : cuisine et salon dans la Casa M-Lidia de RCR Arquitectes.* Quelle des Lichts: Küche und Wohnzimmer in der Casa M-Lidia von RCR Arquitectes.

102/103 Living in a former water tower: the home of Marja Maassen and Jan Moereels. *Habiter dans un ancien château d'eau : chez Marja Maassen et Jan Moereels.* Wohnen in einem ehemaligen Wasserturm: Bei Marja Maassen und Jan Moereels.

104/105 Dining table and work space: Maassen and Moereels' cherry-wood counter. *A la fois table à manger et plan de travail : comptoir en bois de cerisier chez Maassen et Moereels.* Esstisch und Arbeitsplatz zugleich: Die Kirschholztheke bei Maassen und Moereels.

106/107 Halfway between Sydney and Melbourne: a house in Bombala, Australia. *A mi-chemin entre Sydney et Melbourne : maison d'habitation à Bombala, Australie.* Auf halbem Weg zwischen Syndey und Melbourne: Ein Wohnhaus in Bombala, Australien.

108/109 Homage to architecture with a farm-house ambience: living in Bombala, Australia. *Hommage à l'architecture et à l'atmosphère des maisons-fermes : la vie à Bombala, en Australie.* Hommage an Archiketur und Ambiente der Farmhäuser: Leben in Bombala, Australien.

110/111 Unlimited space: living area at the Provençal home of Armand Bartos. *Tout est espace : zone d'habitation dans la maison d'Armand Bartos en Provence.* Alles ist Raum: Wohnbereich im Haus von Armand Bartos in der Provence. *Architect: Claudio Silvestrin*

112/113 Modern mosaic: work of art at Armand Bartos. *Mosaïque moderne : œuvre d'art chez Armand Bartos.* Modernes Mosaik: Kunstwerk bei Armand Bartos. *Architect: Claudio Silvestrin*

114/115 Triangles and rectangles: design concept for the home of Armand Bartos. *Triangles et rectangles : design et concept pour la maison d'Armand Bartos.* Dreiecke und Rechtecke: Design-Konzepte im Haus von Armand Bartos. *Architect: Claudio Silvestrin*

116/117 Hidden behind a white wall: Armand Bartos's kitchen. *Dissimulée derrière une paroi blanche : la cuisine d'Armand Bartos.* Hinter einer weißen Wand verborgen: Armand Bartos Küche. *Architect: Claudio Silvestrin*

118/119 Bathroom with a view: uncluttered at the home of Armand Bartos. *Salle de bains avec vue imprenable : design puriste dans la maison d'Armand Bartos.* Bad mit Ausblick: Puristisches Design im Haus von Armand Bartos. *Architect: Claudio Silvestrin*

120/121 A bathroom in Beauval stone: Simple but beautiful design. *La salle de bains en pierre de Beauval : atmosphère belle et sobre.* Badezimmer aus Beauval-Stein: Schön schlichtes Ambiente. *Architect: Claudio Silvestrin*

122/123 Glacial tones: a loft in the old part of Lucerne, Switzerland. *Tonalités de glacier : dans un loft de la vieille ville de Lucerne.* Gletschertöne: In einem Loft in der Altstadt von Luzern. *Architect: Gus Wüstemann*

124/125 Sculpted storage space: appliances are hidden behind white surfaces. *Espace de rangement sculptural : les ustensiles disparaissent derrière des surfaces blanches.* Skulpturengleicher Stauraum: Geräte verschwinden hinter weißen Flächen. *Architect: Gus Wüstemann*

126/127 Dazzling mountain light interspersed with warmer shades: bathroom in the Lucerne loft. *Tons chauds et luminosité de la montagne : salle de bains du loft de Lucerne.* Warme Nuancen und strahlendes Berglicht: Badezimmer des Lofts in Luzern. *Architect: Gus Wüstemann*

"… I still remember those old lacquered screens – they always fascinated me …"

Eileen Gray

« … Je me rappelle bien ces paravents laqués – ils m'avaient déjà fasciné depuis toujours … »

Eileen Gray

»… Ich erinnere mich noch gut an diese alten Lackwandschirme – sie hatten mich schon immer fasziniert …«

Eileen Gray

DETAILS

Détails Details

NICOLAS SABBATINI, 1594, ROME, 1666-5?,
RÉALISA POUR UNE CRÉATION OUBLIÉE DE CORNEILLE
UN RIDEAU DE SCÈNE SI SAVANT QUE LES ACTEURS
DÉCLAMAIENT DE ZOUER EN OMBRE CHINOISE DERRIÈRE LUI.

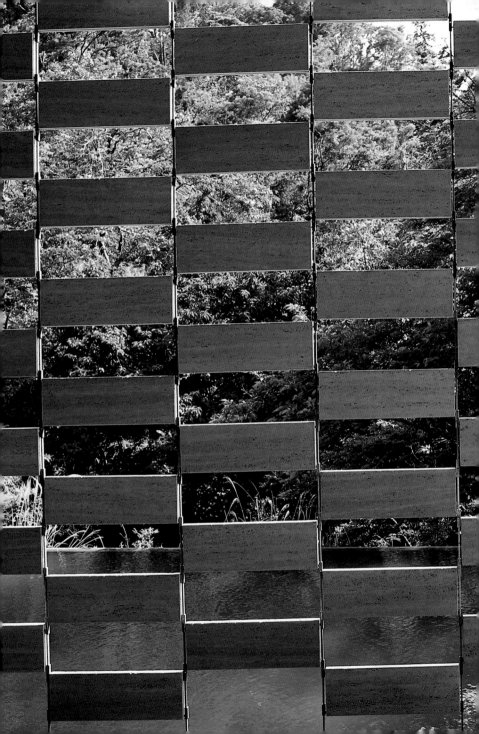

134 Corridor leading to the bedroom: at Farnsworth House. *Passage conduisant à la chambre à coucher : dans la maison Farnsworth.* Durchgang zum Schlafzimmer: Im Farnsworth House. *Architect: Ludwig Mies van der Rohe (1945/50)*

136 Glass façade reaching to the ceiling: Farnsworth House. *Façade vitrée jusqu'au plafond : la maison Farnsworth.* Raumhohe Fensterfronten: Im Farnsworth House. *Architect: Ludwig Mies van der Rohe (1945/50)*

137 By the fire: open fireplace at Farnsworth House. *Tout près du feu : cheminée ouverte dans la maison Farnsworth.* Ganz nahe am Feuer: Offener Kamin im Farnsworth House. *Architect: Ludwig Mies van der Rohe (1945/50)*

138 Art to match the furniture: Casa Luis Barragán in Mexico City. *Mobilier et art, ton sur ton : dans la Casa Luis Barragán à Mexico.* Möbel und Kunst Ton in Ton: In der Casa Luis Barragán in Mexiko City.

140 Clean lines: staircase to the upper floor of Casa Luis Barragán. *Formes claires : l'escalier qui conduit à l'étage supérieur dans la Casa Luis Barragán.* Klare Formen: Treppe zum Obergeschoss der Casa Luis Barragán.

141 Touches of yellow: room with fireplace in the Casa Luis Barragán. *Accents de jaune : dans la salle de la cheminée de la Casa Luis Barragán.* Akzente in Gelb: Im Kaminzimmer der Casa Luis Barragán.

142 A work of art: sharp contrast between light and shadow. *Un chef-d'œuvre : contrastes vifs d'ombres et de lumière solaire.* Ein Kunstwerk: Scharf gezeichnete Kontraste von Sonnenlicht und Schatten. *Architect: Luis Barragán*

144 Long table: dining room designed by Vincent van Duysen. *Table longue : design d'une salle à manger de Vincent van Duysen.* Lange Tafel: Ein Esszimmer, gestaltet von Vincent van Duysen.

145 Design classics: in a house furnished by van Duysen. *Un classique du design : dans une maison aménagée par van Duysen.* Design-Klassiker: In einem vom van Duysen eingerichteten Haus.

146 Heat source: fireplace at the home of John and Catherine Pawson. *Source de chaleur : cheminée dans la maison de John & Catherine Pawson.* Wärmequelle: Kamin im Haus von John & Catherine Pawson.

148 Perfect perspective: narrow staircase in Pawson's house. *Pureté de la perspective : montée d'un escalier étroit chez Pawson.* Perspektive pur: Schmaler Treppenaufgang bei Pawson's.

149 White bathtub: bathroom design by Vincent van Duysen. *Baignoire blanche : design de salle de bains que l'on doit à Vincent van Duysen.* Weiße Wanne: Bad-Design von Vincent van Duysen.

151 Space to work: John & Catherine Pawson's kitchen. *Arrondi les angles : dans la cuisine de John & Catherine Pawson.* Genug Platz um zu arbeiten: In der Küche von John & Catherine Pawson.

152 Splashes of colour: Eames chairs in Hans-Peter Jochum's apartment. *Touches de couleur : chaises Eames dans l'appartement de Hans-Peter Jochum.* Farbtupfer: Eames-Stühle in der Wohnung von Hans-Peter Jochum.

153 Paint instead of tiles: Hans-Peter Jochum's bathroom. *A la place du carrelage, de la laque : dans la salle de bains de Hans-Peter Jochum.* Lack statt Fliesen: Im Bad von Hans-Peter Jochum.

154 Just like standing at a counter: kitchen units in the style of Vincent van Duysen. *Comme un comptoir : ligne de cuisine dans le style de Vincent van Duysen.* Wie eine Theke: Küchenzeile im Stil von Vincent van Duysen.

156 Marbled: a wall of Beauval stone in Armand Bartos's house. *Marbré : un mur Beauval dans la maison d'Armand Bartos.* Marmoriert: Eine Beauval-Wand im Haus von Armand Bartos. *Architect: Claudio Silvestrin*

157 A favourite place: Armand Bartos's stone bathtub. *Coin préféré : la baignoire de pierre d'Armand Bartos.* Lieblingsplatz: Die steinerne Badewanne von Armand Bartos. *Architect: Claudio Silvestrin*

159 Architecture and accessories in perfect harmony: in Armand Bartos's house. *Architecture et accessoires, ton sur ton : chez Armand Bartos.* Architektur und Accessoires Ton in Ton: Bei Armand Bartos. *Architect: Claudio Silvestrin*

160 Tricks of the light: a long corridor in Bartos's house. *Accents de lumière : long couloir dans la maison de Bartos.* Akzente durch Licht: Langer Flur im Haus von Bartos. *Architect: Claudio Silvestrin*

161 Framed by light: narrow staircase by Armand Bartos. *Encadré de lumière : escalier étroit chez Armand Bartos.* Ein Rahmen aus Licht: Schmale Treppe bei Armand Bartos. *Architect: Claudio Silvestrin*

162 Even the wiring is artistic: in Armand Bartos's house. *Câbleart : dans la maison d'Armand Bartos.* Kunst aus Kabeln: Im Haus von Armand Bartos. *Architect: Claudio Silvestrin*

164 All good things come in threes: leading the sweet life in Bombala, Australia. *Jamais deux sans trois : jouir de la vie à Bombala, Australie.* Aller guten Dinge sind drei: Leben und Genießen in Bombala, Australien.

165 In line: candles in a house in Bombala. *Bien alignées : bougies dans la maison de Bombala.* In Reih und Glied: Kerzen in einem Haus in Bombala.

167 In communion with nature: bathroom in Casa M-Lidia, Montagut, Girona. *En lien avec la nature : la salle de bains de la Casa M-Lidia à Montagut, Gérone.* Naturverbunden: Bad der Casa M-Lidia in Montagut, Girona.

168 Linear: kitchen in Tom de Paor's Double House in Dublin. *Linéaire : cuisine dans la maison jumelle de Tom de Paor à Dublin.* Linear: Küche im Double House in Dublin von Tom de Paor.

169 A glimpse into infinity: Tom de Paor's Double House in Dublin. *Comme un regard sur l'éternité : dans la maison jumelle de Dublin.* Wie ein Blick in die Unendlichkeit: Im Double House in Dublin von Tom de Paor.

170 Ice age: glacial atmosphere in the old part of Lucerne. *Âge de glace : ambiance glacier dans un loft de la vieille ville, à Lucerne. Eiszeit: Gletscher-Ambiente in einem Loft in Luzerns Altstadt. Architect: Gus Wüstemann*

172 As smooth as a frozen lake: view of the bathroom in the Lucerne loft. *Lisse comme un lac gelé : coup d'œil dans la salle de bains du loft de Lucerne. So glatt wie ein zugefrorener See: Blick ins Bad des Lofts in Luzern.*

173 "Polar bearskin": accessories in the bedroom of Gus Wüstemann's loft. *« Ours polaire »: accessoires dans la chambre à coucher du loft. »Eisbär«-Accessoires: im Schlafzimmer des Lofts von Gus Wüstemann.*

175 Cleverly concealed cupboard: a Vincent van Duysen design. *Buffet habilement dissimulé : une invention de Vincent van Duysen. Geschickt verborgener Geschirrschrank: Ein Entwurf von Vincent van Duysen.*

176 A clear view of the countryside: seen from the Lotus House. *Vue dégagée sur la nature : depuis la maison Lotus. Freier Blick auf die Natur: Vom Lotus House aus gesehen. Architect: Kengo Kuma*

177 Perfection: this partition wall in the Lotus House appears to float. *Exemplaire : mur de séparation presque flottant, dans la maison Lotus. Mustergültig: Fast freischwebende Trennwand im Lotus House.*

178 Out of thin air: staircase in Kengo Kuma's Lotus House. *Aérien : escalier de la maison Lotus de Kengo Kuma. Wie aus der Luft gegriffen: Treppe in Kengo Kumas Lotus House.*

180 Sleeping in a simple setting: bedroom in the house of the architect Wong. *Dormir dans la sobriété : la maison de l'architecte Wong. Schlafen in schlichter Atmosphäre: Im Haus des Architekten Wong.*

181 Red line: colourful trim at Voon Yee Wong's home in London. *Ligne rouge : bordure colorée chez Voon Yee Wong à Londres. Rote Linie: Farbbordüre bei Voon Yee Wong in London.*

182 Bright red: tea towel on a sideboard designed by Vincent van Duysen. *Rouge vif : serviette sur un sideboard dessiné par Vincent van Duysen. Knallrot: Handtuch auf einem Sideboard, entworfen von Vincent van Duysen.*

184 Soft light: a relaxing corner of the architect Voon Yee-Wong's house. *Pause en bleu : ambiance paisible dans la maison de l'architecte Voon Yee Wong. Blaue Pause: Friedliches Flair im Haus des Architekten Voon Yee Wong.*

185 Misty: the view from a room designed by van Duysen. *Doucement voilé : regard vers l'extérieur depuis une pièce Duysen. Zart verhangen: Blick aus einem von van Duysen gestalteten Zimmer nach draußen.*

187 Spartan but impressive: Tadao Ando's 4x4 House. *Spartiate mais plein d'effet : dans la maison 4x4 de Tadao Ando. Spartanisch und wirkungsvoll zugleich: Im 4x4 House von Tadao Ando.*

Photo Credits

10/11
Getty Images

12/13
akg-images

14/15
akg-images/Erich Lessing

16/17
RIBA Library Photographs Collection

18/19
Nai, Rotterdam

20/21
Getty Images

22/23
Alan Weintraub/Arcaid

24/25
Julius Shulman Photography, Los Angeles, California

26/27
Julius Shulman Photography, Los Angeles, California

28/29
Julius Shulman Photography, Los Angeles, California

30/31
G. E. Kidder Smith/corbis

32/33
Julius Shulman Photography, Los Angeles, California

34/35
Julius Shulman Photography, Los Angeles, California

36/37
akg-images/Florian Profitlich

38/39
Reto Guntli

40/41
Reto Guntli

42/43
Reto Guntli

48/49
Alan Weintraub/Arcaid

50/51
Alan Weintraub/Arcaid

52/53
Alan Weintraub/Arcaid

54/55
Barbara & René Stoeltie

56/57
Barbara & René Stoeltie

58/59
Simon Upton

60/61
Simon Upton

62/63
Simon Upton

64/65
Reto Guntli

66/67
Reto Guntli

68/69
Reto Guntli

70/71
Reto Guntli

72/73
Reto Guntli

74/75
Reto Guntli

76/77
Reto Guntli

78/79
Jean-Luc Laloux

80/81
Jean-Luc Laloux

82/83
Jean-Luc Laloux

84/85
Jean-Luc Laloux

86/87
Reto Guntli

88/89
Reto Guntli

90/91
Deidi von Schaewen

92/93
Deidi von Schaewen

94/95
Deidi von Schaewen

96/97
Morley von Sternberg/Arcaid

98/99
Eugeni Pons/Arcaid

100/101
Eugeni Pons/Arcaid

102/103
Henry Bourne/Architektur & Wohnen

104/105
Henry Bourne/Architektur & Wohnen

106/107
Mads Mogensen & Martina Hunglinger

108/109
Mads Mogensen & Martina Hunglinger

110/111
Deidi von Schaewen

112/113
Deidi von Schaewen

114/115
Deidi von Schaewen

116/117
Deidi von Schaewen

118/119
Deidi von Schaewen

120/121
Deidi von Schaewen

122/123
Bruno Helbling/zapaimages

124/125
Bruno Helbling/zapaimages

126/127
Bruno Helbling/zapaimages

134
Alan Weintraub/Arcaid

136
Alan Weintraub/Arcaid

137
Alan Weintraub/Arcaid

138
Barbara & René Stoeltie

140
Barbara & René Stoeltie

141
Barbara & René Stoeltie

142
Barbara & René Stoeltie

144
Jean-Luc Laloux

145
Jean-Luc Laloux

146
Simon Upton

148
Simon Upton

149
Jean-Luc Laloux

151
Simon Upton

152
Production: Patricia Parinejad, Photo: Eric Laignel

153
Production: Patricia Parinejad, Photo: Eric Laignel

154
Jean-Luc Laloux

156
Deidi von Schaewen

157
Deidi von Schaewen

159
Deidi von Schaewen

160
Deidi von Schaewen

161
Deidi von Schaewen

162
Deidi von Schaewen

164
Mads Mogensen & Martina Hunglinger

165
Mads Mogensen & Martina Hunglinger

167
Eugeni Pons/Arcaid

168
Morley von Sternberg/Arcaid

169
Morley von Sternberg/Arcaid

170
Bruno Helbling/zapaimages

172
Bruno Helbling/zapaimages

173
Bruno Helbling/zapaimages

175
Jean-Luc Laloux

176
Reto Guntli

177
Reto Guntli

178
Reto Guntli

180
Deidi von Schaewen

181
Deidi von Schaewen

182
Jean-Luc Laloux

184
Deidi von Schaewen

185
Jean-Luc Laloux

187
Reto Guntli

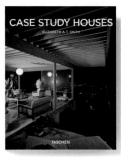
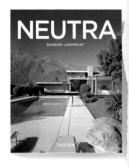

Architecture Now! Vol. 4
Philip Jodidio / Flexi-cover,
576 pp. / € 29.99 / $ 39.99 /
£ 19.99 / ¥ 5.900

Case Study Houses
Elizabeth Smith / Ed. Peter
Gössel / Softcover, 96 pp. /
€ 6.99 / $ 9.99 / £ 4.99 /
¥ 1.500

Richard Neutra
Barbara Lamprecht / Ed. Peter
Gössel / Softcover, 96 pp. /
€ 6.99 / $ 9.99 / £ 4.99 /
¥ 1.500

"Part 4 of this extremely well researched reference book presents the creators and their latest works – from Pawson's monastery to Koolhaas' library" —*Elle Deco*, Munich, on *Architecture Now! Vol. 4*

"Buy them all and add some pleasure to your life."

ICONS